Great Artists

Paul Cézanne

By Iain Zaczek

I0799195

Gareth Stevens Publishing

Please visit our website, www.garethstevens.com. For a free color catalog of all our high-quality books, call toll-free 1-800-542-2595 or fax 1-877-542-2596.

Library of Congress Cataloging-in-Publication Data

Zaczek, Iain.
Paul Cezanne / by Iain Zaczek.
p. cm. — (Great artists)
Includes index.
ISBN 978-1-4824-1216-1 (pbk.)
ISBN 978-1-4824-1244-4 (6-pack)
ISBN 978-1-4824-1502-5 (library binding)
1. Cézanne, Paul, — 1839-1906 — Juvenile literature. 2. Painters — France — Biography — Juvenile literature. I. Zaczek, Iain. II. Title.
ND553.C33 Z33 2015
759.4—d23

Published in 2015 by
Gareth Stevens Publishing
111 East 14th Street, Suite 349
New York, NY 10003

© 2014 Brown Bear Books Ltd

For Brown Bear Books Ltd:
Editorial Director: Lindsey Lowe
Managing Editor: Tim Cooke
Children's Publisher: Anne O'Daly
Design Manager: Keith Davis
Designer: Supriya Sahai
Picture Manager: Sophie Mortimer

Picture Credits
Special thanks to The Art Archive
T=Top, C=Center, B=Bottom, L=Left, R=Right
Cover, ©TheArt Archive/Musee d'Orsay, Paris/Collection Dagli Orti; 4, ©Private Collection/Public Domain; 5, © Shutterstock/Chippix; 6, ©RHL/Art Gallery of New South Wales; 7, ©Shutterstock/Pack-Shot; 8t, ©Shutterstock/Henri Faure; 8b, © Shutterstock/Luca Quadrio; 9, ©Public Domain/Courtauld; 10-11, ©Public Domain/Hermitage; 11tl, ©Shutterstock/Irina Mossina; 11tr, ©Shutterstock/Brandanht; 11bc, ©Thinkstock/Tatyana Tomsickova; 12-13, ©The Art Archive/DeA Picture Library/G. Nimatallah; 14-15, ©The Art Archive/Burrell Collection, Glasgow; 16-17, ©The Art Archive/DeA Picture Library; 18-19, ©The Art Archive/Musee d'Orsay, Paris/Collection Dagli Orti; 21, ©The Art Archive Musee d'Orsay, Paris/Collection Dagli Orti; 22-23, ©The Art Archive/DeA Picture Library; 24-25, ©The Art Archive/Musee d'Orsay, Paris/Collection Dagli Orti; 26-27, ©The Art Archive/DeA Picture Library /M. Carrieri; 27tr, ©The Art Archive/DeA Picture Library.

Brown Bear Books has made every attempt to contact the copyright holder. If anyone has any information please contact licensing@brownbearbooks.co.uk

All artwork: © Brown Bear Books/Supriya Sahai

All rights reserved. No part of this book may be reproduced, stored in a retrieval system, or transmitted in any form or by any means, electronic, mechanical, photocopying, recording, or otherwise, without the prior written permission of the copyright holder.

Manufactured in the United States of America

CPSIA compliance information: Batch #CS15GS. For further information contact Gareth Stevens, New York, New York at 1-800-542-2595.

Contents

Life Story

When Paul Cézanne started to paint and draw, people laughed at his odd pictures. Today he is seen as one of the painters who shaped modern art with his new ideas.

Paul Cézanne was born in Aix-en-Provence in the south of France. Paul's father, Louis-Auguste, was a banker who had once made hats. Paul and his two sisters, Marie and Rose, grew up in a wealthy household. Paul did well at school. One of his close friends was Émile Zola, who would become one of the greatest writers in France. Although Paul's father wanted him to be a lawyer, Paul wanted to be an artist.

Birth name: **Paul Cézanne**

Born: **January 19, 1839, Aix-en-Provence, France**

Died: **October 22, 1906, Aix-en-Provence, France**

Nationality: **French**

Field: **Painting**

Movement: **Post-Impressionism**

Influenced by: **Camille Pissarro**

Self-Portrait
Paul Cézanne, c.1895

BUSINESSMAN Paul's father owned a bank. Paul worked there for a time.

In 1858 Paul began taking drawing lessons. Because his father wanted Paul to become a lawyer, Paul also studied law at university. But he did not enjoy it, and in 1861, his father finally allowed him to give up his law studies.

Moving to Paris

Paul moved to study art in Paris. Émile Zola had also moved to Paris. Paul studied at the Académie Suisse. Anyone could pay to go to classes there. Other students made fun of Paul's drawings. He was shy and found it difficult to make friends. But he did become friendly with Camille Pissarro, who later became a leading Impressionist painter. After a few months in Paris, Paul returned home and took a job in his father's bank.

Famous Paintings:

- ***The House of the Hanged Man*** 1873
- ***The Château of Médan*** 1880
- ***Mont Sainte-Victoire*** 1887
- ***The Card Players*** 1894–95
- ***Woman with a Coffee Pot*** 1895
- ***Lake of Annecy*** 1896
- ***Apples and Oranges*** 1899

If you respect nature, it will always unravel its meaning for you.

Important people

Émile Zola – friend and writer
Camille Pissarro – friend and painter
Claude Monet – friend and painter
Victor Choquet – art collector
Ambroise Vollard – art dealer

Camille Pissarro

Paul's friend Pissarro helped to found the Impressionist movement. He was the only artist who had paintings in all eight exhibitions that the Impressionists held in Paris. He later moved away from the Impressionist style. Like Paul, he painted in a style known as Post-Impressionism.

Try, try again

Paul still wanted to become an artist. He kept disappearing from work to take lessons at the drawing school. In November 1862, he went back to Paris. He tried to get into the best art school, the École des Beaux-Arts but was turned down. He also tried to have one of his pictures accepted by the Paris Salon. This was the official exhibition of the best paintings produced in France. The Salon rejected Paul's painting. Paul would send painting after painting to the Salon. Only one was ever accepted.

In 1869, Paul met a seamstress and artist's model named Hortense Fiquet. In 1872, they had a son and named him Paul. The family could not afford to live in Paris. Instead they moved to a small town nearby named Auvers. Paul's friend Camille Pissarro lived nearby. They often painted together.

A new approach

Paul usually painted portraits and still lifes. But now he followed Pissarro's example and began painting more landscapes. He also painted more like Pissarro's friends, the Impressionists.

"If I think while I'm painting, then whoosh!, everything goes to pieces."

The Impressionists were young artists who painted in new ways. They wanted to paint images of everyday life as it really appeared. In 1874, Paul's paintings were included in the first Impressionist exhibition.

Key places

Aix-en-Provence

Paris

Auvers

Falling out

In 1878, Paul's father stopped sending Paul money. Paul's friend Émile Zola was now a famous writer. He gave Paul money until the two men fell out in 1886. Paul thought Émile had written about him in a story about a failed artist. He never spoke to Émile again.

In 1886, Paul married Hortense. That same year his father died. He left Paul enough money for Paul to stop worrying about it. Now he could paint what he wanted.

CHURCH IN AUVERS
Paul moved to Auvers with Hortense and their son, Paul. It was cheaper to live there than in Paris.

MONT SAINTE-VICTOIRE
Mont Sainte-Victoire is a mountain that rises over the countryside near Aix. The top is very rocky. The mountain was one of Paul's favorite subjects. He painted it more than 60 times.

Middle age

Paul was now middle-aged. For the next 20 years he worked hard to develop a painting style. He spent most of his time in Aix. Hortense and their son lived mostly in Paris, and Paul visited them from time to time. In 1894, he also visited the Impressionist painter Claude Monet at his home at Giverny in northeast France.

Paul was largely forgotten by the art world of Paris until 1895. Pissarro asked an art dealer named Ambroise Vollard to organize an exhibition of about 150 of Paul's paintings. Many younger artists saw his work for the first time. They included Pablo Picasso and Georges Braque. Paul became a hero to them.

Paul spent most of his time in Aix-en-Provence, where he had been born.

Ambroise Vollard was a famous art dealer in Paris. He helped many artists sell their paintings. The exhibition he organized helped make Paul famous as an artist.

Growing old

Paul was healthy for most of his life. In 1890, however, he began to suffer from a condition called diabetes. By 1900, he had become quite sick. But he still worked in his studio or outdoors in the countryside around Aix.

In 1906, Paul was painting outdoors when he was caught in a sudden rainstorm. He collapsed. A week later, on October 22, 1906, he died of pneumonia. By this time his fame was growing. An exhibition of his work was held a year later. It was received with praise, and showed that Paul had been one of the leading artists of his time.

How Cézanne Painted

Paul Cézanne was a Post-Impressionist. These painters learned to use Impressionist techniques but then developed their own style.

Paul learned about Impressionism from his friend Camille Pissarro. Pissarro was one of the leaders of the movement. He persuaded Paul to try painting outdoors and suggested he used lighter colors. Paul's pictures were included in two Impressionist exhibitions. But they were not very popular. Paul always remained on the edges of the Impressionist group.

Impressionism

Pissarro and the Impressionists painted scenes of everyday life. Their pictures often looked unfinished compared to paintings by earlier artists such as Jacques-Louis David. Pissarro painted this street in Paris in 1897.

Simple subjects
Paul used subjects like fruit for his paintings.

Simple shapes
Paul looked for bold, simple shapes, like circles.

Paul did not like the way the Impressionists painted. They tried to paint things that changed quickly, such as light reflections and shadows. Paul said he wanted his paintings to appear more solid. He said paintings should be "like the art of the museums."

Paul worked very slowly. He built up his pictures using tiny touches of paint. He did not mind changing the shape or color of things to create the image he had in mind. He chose simple subjects, such as landscapes, portraits, or still lifes (collections of objects). But he wanted his subjects to seem as impressive as the heroic scenes shown in old paintings. "I want to astonish Paris with an apple," he once said.

Paul believed that something as simple as an apple could be as important as a scene from history if painted well enough.

The House of the Hanged Man

This painting marked a big moment in Paul's early career as an artist. It was the first painting he ever sold. It was displayed in the first Impressionist exhibition in Paris in 1874.

The painting shows Auvers-sur-Oise, a town in northern France, not far from Paris. Paul painted it when he was living in Auvers with his family in 1873. His friend Camille Pissarro lived nearby. They used to paint outdoors together. The painting's title is dramatic. The owner of the house was said to have killed himself. But this story might not have been true.

In the Frame

- The original painting of *The House of the Hanged Man* is 21.5 inches high (55 cm) and 26 inches (66 cm) wide.
- It was the first painting Paul ever sold.

Paul signed this picture. That was unusual and showed he thought it was finished. He often kept working on paintings and so never signed them.

This roof is painted with thick dabs of browns, greens, and yellows. The green makes it look as if moss or mold is growing on the roof.

The paint is very thick. Paul added new layers on top of paint that had already dried. This gives the picture a grainy texture.

The trees in front of the house draw the eye toward the building. This was a technique Paul learned from his friend Camille Pissarro.

CEZANNE'S

Palette of the picture

The Château of Médan

Paul painted this picture around 1880 during a visit with his friend, Émile Zola. The writer owned a house in Médan, a village just outside Paris.

Paul used to row Zola's boat across the Seine River to get this view of the local château, or castle. He did not try to paint an exact copy of the view. He wanted his picture to look more interesting. The first owner of the picture was the Post-Impressionist artist Paul Gauguin. He liked the parallel brushstrokes that were all painted going in the same direction. Gauguin said they reminded him of stitches in silk.

These towers are the 15th-century château. Because Paul wanted to include the château, he did not have room to include all of Zola's house on the right-hand side of the picture.

In the Frame

The original painting of *The Château of Médan* is 23.25 inches (59.1 cm) tall and 28.5 inches (72.4 cm) wide.

The leaves, the riverbank, and the sky are all painted with even, diagonal brushstrokes.

The trees stand in a neat line. Paul Gauguin said they reminded him of a row of tin soldiers.

The riverbank is marked with a thick, unbroken line. There are other strong lines in the picture, such as the roofs of the houses.

CEZANNE'S

Palette of the picture

Mont Sainte-Victoire

The mountain of Sainte-Victoire was just a few miles from Paul's hometown of Aix-en-Provence. The mountain became one of his favorite subjects. He painted it more than 60 times.

This is one of Paul's early paintings of the mountain. He painted it in about 1887 from a viewpoint near his family home. Paul wanted to study the mountain and valley in close detail. In later paintings he painted the landscape as very simple shapes. His last paintings of the mountain were almost like abstract art, and quite unreal.

Some leaves do not appear to be attached to the branches. Was Paul trying to show them shaking in the breeze?

CEZANNE'S

Palette of the picture

In the Frame

The original painting of *Mont Sainte-Victoire* is 26.4 inches (67 cm) tall and 36.2 inches (92 cm wide).

Paul uses soft pinks and blues for the mountain in the distance. The rest of the landscape has stronger colors.

This viaduct carried the local railroad. In his later paintings of the mountain Paul left out this sort of detail.

A young poet named Joachim Gasquet liked this painting. Paul was so pleased that he signed it and gave it to him.

The Card Players

In the early 1890s, Paul painted a series of paintings of men playing cards. The men had worked for Paul's father in Aix. The man with the pipe was a gardener named père, or "father," Alexandre.

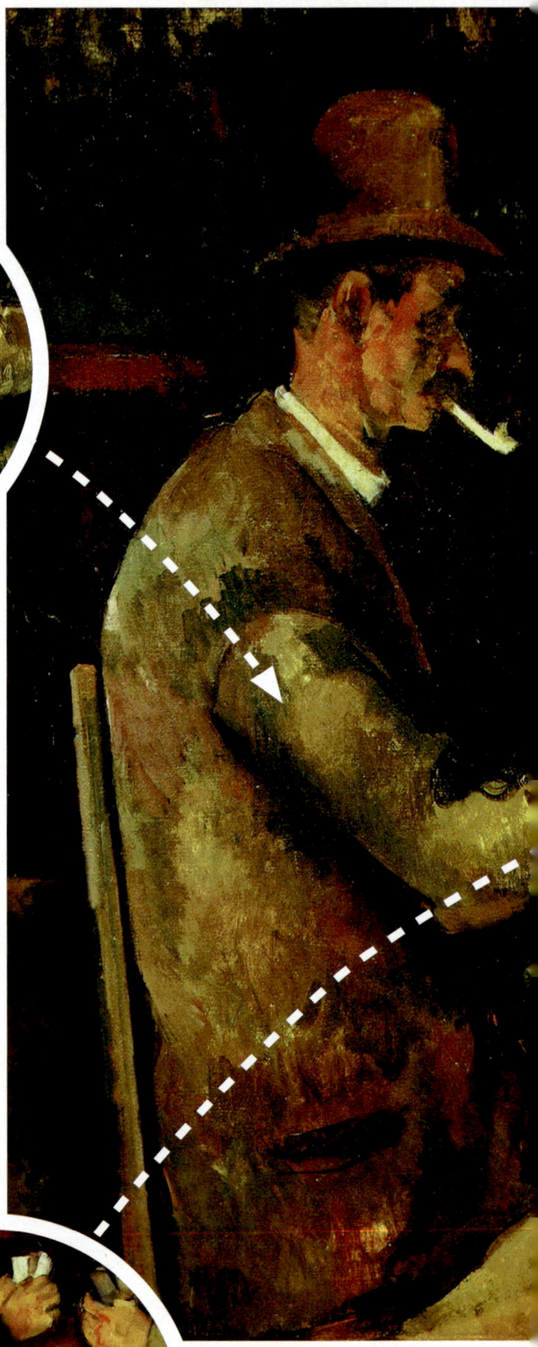

This man's jacket is painted in patches of browns and greys. In places the bare canvas can be seen through the paint.

Artists had often painted pictures of cardplayers. Their paintings had a message. They were meant to show people that gambling was bad. But Paul's picture does not have a message. He just liked the stillness of the scene as the men study their cards. He paints them as if they are in a still life.

Paul does not show what cards the men have. He is more interested in showing the stillness of the scene.

This bottle is carefully positioned. It divides the picture exactly in half.

In the Frame

- The original painting of *The Card Players* is 18 inches (45.7 cm) tall and 22.4 inches (57 cm) wide.
- Cézanne painted men playing cards five times during the early 1890s.

CEZANNE'S

Palette of the picture

On the left, the tablecloth and the man's seat are straight. On the right, the tablecloth and the man's back and shoulders are slanted.

Woman with a Coffee Pot

Paul painted this portrait around 1895. We do not know who the woman is. She was probably a maid or another servant from the Cézanne family home in Aix-en-Provence.

Paul liked painting portraits. He thought that painting faces was one of the most important tasks of an artist. He would probably have done more portraits, but he had trouble finding models. This was partly because he was shy with people. It was also because he worked very slowly. The posing sessions were very difficult for his models.

The woman's face has no expression. Perhaps she was bored after sitting still for so long. Other models said Paul treated them like objects in a still life**.**

In the Frame

- The original painting of *Woman with a Coffee Pot* is 51.2 inches (130 cm) tall and 38 inches (96.5 cm) wide.
- Cézanne does not try to tell us anything about the woman's personality.

CEZANNE'S Palette of the picture

The painting has a strong line running up the center. It begins with the central fold in the woman's dress and continues up through the parting in her hair.

The coffee pot is seen from quite a low angle, but the cup and saucer are seen from above.

The woman's hands are large and rough. This suggests she is used to doing work around the house.

The Lake of Annecy

Paul painted this picture in 1896 while he was on holiday with his family at Talloires in the mountains near the French border with Switzerland.

Paul thought the town was pretty, but he found it boring. He painted this picture to keep himself busy. But he did not paint the lake in a very pretty way. Instead, he showed the landscape as being quite dark. The painting has a threatening feeling. Paul made a number of sketches in Talloires, but he completed the painting at his studio in Aix.

Most of the painting is done in cold blues and greens. The brighter colors on the tree trunk and château suggest the warmth of morning sunshine.

In the Frame

- The original painting of *The Lake of Annecy* is 25.5 inches (65 cm) tall and 31.9 inches (81 cm) wide.
- Paul saw landscape in terms of shapes like cylinders and spheres.

Paul often used a large tree to frame his scene. The two dark, diagonal sections at the top of the canvas are branches of the tree on the left.

Paul painted the mountains as overlapping triangles that block out the sky.

The reflection of the tower is just a series of shapes in the water. It is not quite straight, but Paul did not worry about things like that.

CEZANNE'S

Palette of the picture

Apples and Oranges

Paul liked to paint still lifes. His early still lifes were quite ordinary. By the time he painted this picture in 1899, they had become more full and detailed.

Paul took care with how he arranged the objects. Most still lifes were very "still." But Paul's display looks as if it could collapse at any moment. He used draped cloth as the setting. The viewer has to look very closely to understand what the picture shows. The edge of the table is hidden, and there are odd angles everywhere.

This plate is tilted at an angle. Paul sometimes used wooden blocks to prop up objects to create this effect.

In the Frame

- The original painting of *Still Life with Apples and Oranges* is 29.1 inches (74 cm) tall and 36.6 inches (93 cm) wide.
- The painting is one of a series of six showing similar subjects.

The fruit dish shows how Paul uses different viewpoints in the same painting. The stand is shown from the side, but the bowl is seen from above.

This jug appears in several of Paul's still lifes. It has a flower pattern that is easy to recognize.

CEZANNE'S

Palette of the picture

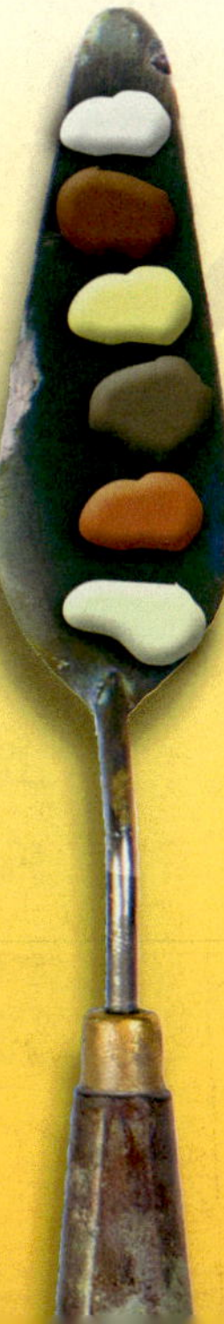

A single apple lies in the middle of the picture. Paul liked painting apples, partly because they did not lose their color too quickly.

What Came Next?

Today Paul Cézanne is often called "the father of modern art." At the start of his career, however, people often laughed at his pictures.

In 1895, Ambroise Vollard held an exhibition of Paul's paintings. For the first time, people began to appreciate his work. Young artists admired how he painted. In the early 20th century, Paul influenced two important groups of painters: the Fauves and the Cubists. The Fauves were a group of French painters. Their name meant "wild beasts." They liked the feeling Paul put into his pictures and the way he applied his paint thickly. The leading Fauve was Henri Matisse. He owned four of Paul's pictures. He said they cheered him up.

Famous Cubists

- **Georges Braque**
- **Robert Delaunay**
- **Juan Gris**
- **Fernand Léger**
- **Pablo Picasso**

Gris's painting seems to show different sides of the objects at the same time.

Juan Gris
Still Life: The Table, 1914.

Delaunay shows Paris as a series of shapes around the Eiffel Tower.

Robert Delaunay
Windows Open Simultaneously, 1911.

Paul had an even bigger influence on the Cubists. They included painters like Pablo Picasso, Georges Braque, Juan Gris, and Robert Delaunay. They liked the way Paul used more than one viewpoint in a picture. They also copied the way he painted nature as a series of simple shapes. That was one of their main techniques. They were called Cubists because they often painted objects as a series of cubes.

How to Paint Like Cézanne

Paul Cézanne had a special way of seeing things. It can be fun to try and see if you can paint everyday things in a different way, too.

WHAT YOU'LL NEED:

- a piece of cloth and some fruit
- a pencil
- thick white paper or cardboard
- small brushes
- acrylic paints

1.

Put some cloth on a flat surface. Arrange two or three pieces of fruit in an interesting shape.

2.

Use a pencil to lightly sketch the outline of the fruit. Use simple shapes, such as circles, squares, and triangles. The shapes can overlap each other. You can even draw parts of the shapes you cannot see. Imagine that the shapes are solid, as if they are different shaped building blocks.

3.

You should have straight and curved lines dividing your drawing into shapes. Start painting the shapes. Try not to paint over the lines. You can add unusual colors if you like, such as blue to a part of a banana that is in shadow.

4.

You should end up with a patchwork of different colors. Now use other colors to paint over the pencil lines.

5.

Painting parts of shapes that you would not be able to see in real life was an important part of Cubism. Cézanne's work was important for the development of this type of modern art.

Timeline

- **1839:** Born in Aix-en-Provence, France.
- **1858:** Starts taking drawing lessons.
- **1861:** Studies art for a few months in Paris but returns home.
- **1862:** Moves to Paris to become an artist.
- **1872:** Moves with his family to a town just outside Paris.
- **1874:** Enters his paintings in the first Impressionist exhibition.
- **1886:** Falls out with his friend Émile Zola.
- **1886:** Inherits a fortune when his father dies.
- **1895:** Has an exhibition in Paris organized by Ambroise Vollard.
- **1906:** Dies of pneumonia in Aix.

Glossary

abstract: A kind of painting that does not try to represent real objects.

allowance: A regular sum of money given to a person to pay their expenses.

canvas: A strong cloth used as a surface for painting.

diabetes: A medical condition that makes people very thirsty and ill.

palette: The range of colors an artist uses in a particular painting.

Post-Impressionist: A style of painting that followed Impressionism. Its name means "After Impressionism."

sketch: A rough drawing usually made as preparation for a large painting.

still life: A painting or drawing of a collection of objects, which often includes fruit or flowers.

studio: A place where an artist paints.

traditional: Something that has been done in the same way for a long time.

viaduct: A bridge that carries a road or railroad.

viewpoint: The place where someone stands to look at something.

Further information

BOOKS

Connolly, Sean. *The Life and Works of Paul Cézanne.* Heinemann Library, 2007.

Harris, Nathaniel. *Paul Cézanne* (Artists in their World). Franklin Watts, 2006.

Mis, Melody S. *Paul Cézanne* (Meet the Artist). PowerKids Press, 2007.

Noble, Marty. *Color Your Own Cézanne Paintings.* Dover Children's, 2007.

Sheen, Barbara. *Paul Cézanne* (Eye on Art). Lucent Books, 2012.

Tracy, Kathleen. *Paul Cézanne* (Art Profiles for Kids). Mitchell Lane Publishers, 2007.

Wood, Alix. *Paul Cézanne* (Artists Through the Ages). Windmill Books, 2013.

MUSEUMS

You can see Paul's famous paintings from this book in these museums:

The House of the Hanged Man
Musée d'Orsay, Paris, France

The Château of Médan
Burrell Collection, Glasgow, UK

Mont Sainte-Victoire
Courtauld Institute of Art, London, UK

The Card Players
Musée d'Orsay, Paris, France

Woman with a Coffee Pot
Musée d'Orsay, Paris, France

The Lake of Annecy
Courtauld Institute of Art, London, UK

Apples and Oranges
Musée d'Orsay, Paris, France

WEBSITES

http://www.nationalgallery.org.uk/artists/paul-cezanne
A site from the National Gallery, London, with links to Paul's paintings.

http://www.metmuseum.org/metmedia/kids-zone/start-with-art/cezannes-astonishing-apples
Metropolitan Museum of Art site about "Cézanne's Astonishing Apples."

http://www.artble.com/artists/paul_cezanne
Artble site about Paul and his paintings.

http://www.biography.com/people/paul-cézanne-9542036
The story of Paul's life on a page from biography.com.

Publisher's note to educators and parents: Our editors have carefully reviewed these websites to ensure that they are suitable for students. Many websites change frequently, however, and we cannot guarantee that a site's future contents will continue to meet our high standards of quality and educational value. Be advised that students should be closely supervised whenever they access the Internet.

Index